YESHUA

The Name Above All Names

Douglas DoNascimento

YESHUA:
The Name Above All Names
Author: Douglas DoNascimento

All rights reserved. No part of this book may be reproduced or transmitted in any form or by any means, electronic or mechanical, including photocopying, recording or by any information storage and retrieval system, without written permission from the author, except for the inclusion of brief quotations in a review.

Unless otherwise noted, Scripture taken from the HOLY BIBLE, NEW INTERNATIONAL VERSION Copyright © 1973, 1978, 1984 International Bible Society. Used by permission of Zondervan Bible Publishers.

While the author has made every effort to provide accurate references and Web addresses at the time of publication, neither the publisher nor the author assumes any responsibility for errors or for changes that occur after publication.

Copyright © 2020 by Douglas DoNascimento
ISBN: 978-1-7321916-0-0

Design & Layout by: Douglas DoNascimento
Published by:
    Briggs & Schuster
    BSA.IM

Printed in the United States of America

CONTENTS

Introduction vii

PART ONE

The Many Jesuses 1
   The Jesus of the Art 2
   The Jesus of Literature 5
   The Jesus of Culture 7
   The Zealot Jesus 8
   The Mythological Jesus 10
   The Hollywood Jesus 11
   The Extraterrestrial Jesus 14
   The Jesus of Politics 15
   The Jesus of Religion 16
   The Jesus of the Bible 17

PART TWO

Discovering Yeshua 21
   The Meaning 25
   The Man and His Jewishness 30
   The Perception 38
   The Essence of His Purpose 41

REFERENCES 47

INTRODUCTION

How is it possible that one man from a small town could have changed the course of history in just three years?

When I initially became inspired to write my first Christian book, I just knew it was going to be about Jesus, but I didn't realize that there were so many books out there with Jesus as the topic. Although, it makes sense, doesn't it?

Jesus is inspirational; his story has spread from the bible and into other forms of literature, movies, music, etc. He's the central figure in Christianity, the most important figure as the Messiah - but he's misunderstood and often misinterpreted.

Did you know there are more books written about Jesus than any other personality in the history of the world?

Of course, Jesus has changed the world, and over the last two thousand years has raised an absolute massive number of followers. His effect and the stories about him are so far-reaching that he's affected modern culture across the planet.

He's more than a biblical figure for a lot of people and we're going to explore that in more depth herein.

This book does not intend or claim to be an all inclusive book about Jesus and all the facets which have been created regarding him - such a book would simply be impossible to write, after all.

Instead, this book outlines the many jesuses out there and the Biblical account of the son of the Almighty God. My aim is to explore the highlights, the many variations of Jesus, with the primary goal of identifying those facets which are merely projections of modern culture or literature, and to find and focus on the Righteous One.

I won't pretend to know everything about Jesus, the fact is, no one does. By pure definition, no one knows everything about anything. My goal with this book is to assist you when you talk about Jesus with other people. Eliminate the confusion and realize that accuracy is important when talking about the LORD. Also, this book should help you stay aware of the many jesuses and ensure that you, and the person you are talking to, are on the same page, talking about the same person.

Accuracy is important when talking about the LORD.

My wish is that this small book will help you to minimize all of the confusion about who Jesus truly is.

This is your demystification process: Over the course of this book, together we will peel back the layers of what you have learned about Jesus, finding the real man beneath all the myths and depictions which have been fed to you through the years.

Rabbi Douglas

PART ONE
The Many Jesuses

Like the complex four-dimensional puzzle it is, I will present you with the pieces and show you how they fit together.

Many of these characters do overlap and that's what makes this a 4-D puzzle. It all depends on the angle from which you're viewing each iteration of Jesus. In some cases, they may look alike, in others behave alike, however, their distinctive incarnations are what landed them into their corresponding buckets.

But why another book about Jesus? Don't we already have enough books about him? Haven't all the theologians already dissected his life in detail? Why regurgitate what others have already stated?

If you asked yourself those questions, we are on the same page - pun intended.

During my research, I read many pieces of information about this subject, yet I couldn't find one book that addressed the many facets in quite this way. Basically, this book is not your all-inclusive "guide to Jesus", the Bible is the only guide we need for that. It is, instead, aimed at uncovering the Jesus you have in your psyche, which may or may not be the true Jesus, and allowing you to reflect on who the biblical Jesus really is.

The Jesus of the Art

Jesus has been depicted in art countless times, whether in paintings or sculptures, or in colored glass. From museums to churches to homes, there are countless representations of his form. This type of symbolism was first used to tell the story with images, so people that couldn't read could understand about Jesus. Unfortunately, many believed that the art was a historical caption of real events, therefore, internalizing in their minds a scene and a Jesus that was meant to be purely an artistic creation created to tell a story.

This Jesus is the most colorful of them all and has good intent drawn right into him.

After all, artists have portrayed Jesus more than any other character in the history of humanity. While their intent may have been good, the depictions can be misleading.

In some cases, the enemy of truth (the devil) has used this character, and too many people worship this facet as the only and true Jesus, when that's not the case. Because it's so easy to confuse this Jesus with the true Jesus, many who do worship him in this particular facet don't really know him or understand what he stands for as described in the Holy Bible.

Probably the most famous depiction of Jesus is one with peony blue eyes and straight hair - very clean cut and neat, with robes and usually a halo around his head.

While there's nothing wrong with admiring and

depicting Jesus, you must understand that these pictures are exactly that – pictures. They are not the true representation of Jesus and what he stands for. They are simply images, often influenced by the artist's own perceptions.

Another example of this would be the Holy Resurrection[3] an image painted by Nana Quparadze which was an image painted in the Georgian style and depicts Jesus as a dark-haired clean man that you are most likely familiar with.

It's important to distinguish the difference between the real Jesus and these drawn or painted versions of the man.

For instance, a creepier 'version' of Jesus was created by Leonardo Da Vinci - note, this is probably the most famous one, and that's what makes it so disturbing.

The story goes that Da Vinci had a homosexual friend or partner, Cesare Borgia, who was the illegitimate son of Pope Alexander VI. Da Vinci thought that his boyfriend, Cesare, had such kind eyes that he would make a fantastic representation of Jesus.

The people of that time - and many today - have been deceived by this wickedness. In fact, this portrayal is so revered and well-known, that the painting itself was auctioned off in 2017 for 450.3 million dollars[1].

If this story about Cesare Borgia is true, then it is clearly a plot from Lucifer to have good-hearted people worshipping wickedness rather than the true son of God. By human standards, a genius move.

You can almost hear Lucifer through this gesture: "If you want to worship him, worship this image instead."

Truly wicked and evil.

Now, we know that God picked ten commandments - his laws - by which we should live our lives. One of these commandments was the following:

> *"You shall not make for yourself an image in the form of anything in heaven above or on the earth beneath or in the waters below. You shall not bow down to them or worship them..."*
> **Exodus 20:4-5**

That seems very clear and to the point. Quite simply put, don't do it. The biblical direction for how we are to worship the Lord Jesus is "in the Spirit and in truth" John 4:23-24. And never prostrated before an image created by man.

Don't create art and worship it. Don't worship the image of Jesus as others have drawn him. Think about it this way – your relationship with Jesus is personal, it is meant to be true and internal, and someone else's drawing of him cannot possibly represent the truth of your personal relationship with him.

Wipe the image of that Jesus - whichever has taken a seat inside your thoughts - from your memory. That would be the path, and that is what it is printed in those ten commandments.

The Jesus of art was created with its commercial angle in mind just like many other man-made gods.

This one is sold with or without the cross and many times just as the empty cross itself. Yes, even the cross as a piece of jewelry can be an idol in its own right.

It's akin to someone murdering your brother and you buying a miniature copy of the gun or knife and hanging it around your neck or putting it somewhere else as a reminder that it was the instrument that killed your brother.

This is probably the touchiest of all of the objects of worship because it is so vastly accepted and embraced culturally. Notwithstanding its wide presence in society, it is a product of art and a creation of artists who saw objects as conduits to worship and the people liked it.

The adoption is universal; the cross has represented Christians for over 2000 years and many were killed under it through the crusades. Many justify worshiping the cross, the empty cross, or through the cross, and the Jesus of art lives on.

Consider these commercial aspects when considering your view of Jesus. Can something which has been sold and bought, which is used to create profit, really be the truth behind the name?

The Jesus of Literature

There is a similarity between the Jesus of Art and the Jesus of Literature: those who created these images of him, both in writing and in drawn form, most likely had the best of intentions. Once again, these iterations of Jesus cannot possibly encompass the truth of him.

They come from the mind of individuals who see him in one particular way. One of the most interesting things about this character is that most of his life is claimed to have been "borrowed" from other historical characters, myths, and the folklore of cultures surrounding Israel.

There are plenty of books which are about Jesus or which include representations of Jesus. The Jesus of literature is the one created to feed most of, if not all the other characters. He is, in short, the supporting actor. An example of this is how he is referred to on the Quran as "Isa" - A prophet smaller than Muhammad.

He validates some truths and questions others. It's the product of man's imagination and opinion. The loftiest idea in literature and the highest personality in philosophy.

For instance, Jesus has been used in short science-fiction stories which predict what he would be like upon return to earth. One such story portrayed him smoking, drinking, acting as Jesus surely wouldn't in the second coming.

Some books portray him in a nonfiction sense, but are still an interpretation of him on a base level. With so many different opinions and portrayals of Jesus, it can be difficult to decide which Jesus is the real one. Which Jesus should you worship?

Quite simply, the one presented in the Holy Bible.

"I am the way and the truth and the life. No one comes to the Father except through me."
John 14:6

I encourage you to read the bible and compare the Jesus presented with the Jesus the world understand. You will be surprised how much distortion has been inserted into the truth and how many lies you will have to unlearn.

The eventual presentation of the true Jesus in this book is an attempt to show the deity witnessed by thousands of people and written about in each of the 66 books of the Bible.

The Jesus of the Culture

Culture is how Jesus has been perceived by humans over the course of several centuries. This character is highly influenced by customary beliefs, social norms and people's values. Naturally, the Jesus of Culture has changed over the course of time.

Let's talk about Israel and Jerusalem. In particular, let's observe the modern culture associated with Jesus.

Many go to Israel seeking to see the place where Jesus walked, lived, and preached. Indeed, when I started writing this book, I had to take a trip there to see it all and immerse myself in the subject of this book from "ground zero."

Jerusalem, Nazareth, and Bethlehem are associated with the Son of the Almighty God. But often these places are used to promote falsities designed to replace the Messiah with the Jesus of Culture and commerce. So, if you find yourself worshiping the land of Israel you need to rethink *who* you are following.

Don't get me wrong, the place is beautiful and a blessing to humanity. It's full of important history. But, it must not be worshiped.

The place where the Messiah became flesh, lived, died, and resurrected should not be worshiped. Instead, we must worship the LORD himself and embrace His Son, His Word, His grace and truth.

> *"The Word became flesh and made his dwelling among us. We have seen his glory, the glory of the one and only Son, who came from the Father, full of grace and truth."*
> **John 1:14**

The Jesus of culture include characters promoted by some of the richest televangelists. This Jesus is based on a pantheistic philosophy which states that there are many roads to God and many roads to Jesus. These are some of the easiest Jesuses to spot, since all you have to do is follow the money.

This cultural Jesus is perhaps the most powerful lie of them all and it is, in fact, a noose; a trap that many have fallen into and have been blinded by it. There is nothing wrong with being rich or a televangelist; the issue is the commercialization of a Gospel that was given to us by God for free and we should give it to one another for free - no strings attached. Period.

The commercialization of the Jesus of culture have given birth to the "gospel of me" and the "prosperity gospel" moviment and its wickedness. The misleading nature of this fake gospel enables those who are not true followers of Christ to take advantage of those who are good-hearted and are truly seeking Him out.

The Zealot Jesus

Mostly a fighter, this Jesus is a very confused character. His preaching doesn't match his actions and he is more of a "freedom fighter" and activist than the legitimate son of God and Savior of the world.

This view is mostly influenced by the way Muslims see Jesus from the lens of the Quran. Their prophet's warrior-like persona have clearly and strongly rubbed off on this character. This Jesus was a prophet and not the son of the Almighty God or Allah. In the case of this Jesus, it's important to understand that when referring to god they are not referring to the Almighty God (Yahweh), they are referring to Allah (Al'Lah) and as you probably already know, Allah is not the name of a person, but rather it is a title that literally translates as "the god" and has been applied mostly to the ancient moon god or as it is also know "the god of the moon."

Back in 2014, an Iranian professor of creative writing at the University of California, Riverside wrote a book called "Zealot" (not a recommended book for many reasons). In one of his interviews about his book, he claimed that he was a Christian who converted to Islam. Red flag!

Let's get one thing straight – no actual believer in Yahweh has ever converted to anything else.

It is possible, however, to refer to a "conversion" as a change of a membership to a club, a group or religion. But in that case, there was never an actual relationship with Yeshua. So, the author of the zealot book is not alone in portraying this character as he does.

Many have claimed the position that Jesus was rightfully crucified because of politics, crime and other variables that fit the Muslim narrative of a warrior/activist mythical character. Nevertheless, the typical regurgitated claims confuse the Jesus of religion with the zealot activists of the time. This is a typical mistake by Islamists as they bundle religion and politics to make their case for a revolutionary activist god.

The history-channel, CNN, and many other networks, push these characters at least once a year. There is always a "new finding" and a load of nonsense from people that have never had a relationship with the living God. To the secular profane media "truth" is relative, therefore, it is not truth at all.

In this portrayal of the zealot Jesus, the media "new discoveries" and the dissections by the "experts" often come from a place driven by ulterior motives, the desire to push a narrative and a genuine lack of a personal relationship with the Son of the One true God.

"By their fruit you will recognize them."
Matthew 7:16

The Mythological Jesus

This is probably the most overlapped Jesus character.

It is comprised of bits and pieces of the many other Jesuses and it is packaged into mysticism, occultism, and tradition. This character has confused most people into believing in him, and often his followers are so hypnotized by the traditions of their religion that they don't care about the real Jesus. They don't want to meet Him or have anything to do with Him.

This Jesus is mostly known by the imprint that he left on the veil cloth given to him by saint Veronica. In this mythological story, Jesus face became imprinted on Veronica's veil during this event. The linen cloth known as the Shroud of Turin is also questionable. Let's dive in.

Once upon a time, there was a man named Jesus, he was carrying his cross on the way to Golgotha and fell several times. During one of these falling episodes, a woman named Veronica, full of compassion, wiped his face with a cloth and at that moment his face was imprinted on the cloth and the cloth became the center of worship for many pilgrims. As tradition goes, the veil possessing the grace of God was able to quench thirst, cure blindness, and even raise the dead.

The Shroud of Turin, however, is still touted as the very shroud which Jesus was wrapped in prior to his resurrection. In fact, some believe that scientific tests of the blood residues on the shroud proves this mystery.

In recent years, another group of highly-qualified individuals has found that the samples of 'blood' on this shroud, might not be blood at all, but paint[4].

The point here is to deter you from placing too much stock in the myths surrounding these fake stories of Jesus but to get to know the real man. Soon we'll touch on who he truly is, and who he is to you.

The Hollywood Jesus

If I ask you to name a few movies which involve Jesus, I'm sure you'd be able to rattle off a few. In fact, there are even children's TV shows which revolve around him as a character - no doubt influencing how children connect with Him from a young age.

Let's name a few:

- Ben Hur
- Jesus Christ SuperStar
- Fireproof
- Son of Man
- The Great Commandment
- The Last Temptation of Christ

The list goes on and on, dating back to the very beginning of the film industry. In some of these movies, Jesus is not the main 'star' so to speak; he's simply the driving force behind decision making. Nonetheless, this is still a depiction of him.

This character - Jesus of Hollywood - is for sure one of the most famous Jesuses as Hollywood has made billions selling his story in many different ways, over and over again. This Jesus is both famous and infamous as the film directors and writers always transfer their own biases to the personality of this character.

One Jesus might seem like the zealot (and this is where the characters of Jesus can very easily overlap) and another might provide that clean-cut image we discussed in the Jesus of Art. The Jesus of Literature plays a role here too, as those writing about him in screenplays place their own opinions and beliefs about him on paper. The Mythological Jesus appears in documentaries about the Shroud of Turin, thus showing yet another overlap between the Jesus of Hollywood and the other depictions mentioned.

It is important for you to understand that the portrayals of the Hollywood Jesus are just creative material designed by man. Some are lies, and most carry biased opinions designed to instigate emotion.

This Jesus embodies most of the lies, half-truths, and mistakes. This character's mother was a woman named Mary and she rode to Bethlehem on a donkey, three kings followed a star and came to visit the newborn baby Jesus.

He was born surrounded by cows, sheep, dogs, cats, rats, chickens... you name it. This guy had a very localized life, in Africa, he was as black as Kunta Kinte, and in Sweden, he was as white as snow. His personality changes like the wind and morphs into whatever the locals want it to be.

People feel very comfortable with this Jesus, as he doesn't require anything from you. Instead, he is all love and acceptance. You don't need to change for this character - he will change himself for you. He is a permissible god for many and he will never judge or let anyone judge you. This guy is cool and, as a good entertainer, he can also sing and dance.

He's there for your entertainment and for your pleasure, or as some churches present him, for "innertainment." He will accept your drug use, your drinking problem and your rendezvous with prostitutes because he does the same – he's a malleable god that you can shape into your life without any personal change.

The Jesus of Hollywood - and his overlap with the Jesuses of Culture, Art, Myth, and History - is an interesting and colorful character. He tends to come to your aid much like a new age butler or genie. Regardless of your behavior and choices, he is always there to serve you.

This representation is riddled with half-truths and flat-out lies and is mostly about your feelings. He's always ready to please you, and, much like Batman's butler Alfred, he may give you his opinion, but if you say "no," he will support you in whatever you want.

In essence, he is always there as your helper and enabler. Typically portrayed as a blond blue-eyed guy. He looks nothing like a person born in Bethlehem, Israel, but rather his looks are more 'in' and 'cool' with his straight hair and all. Scientists have not yet confirmed his virgin birth and there are doubts about his resurrection. They have, however, validated that once there was a man born in Israel with the name Jesus.

Let me be clear - The Son of the Almighty God is not any of the above jesuses. He is not here to entertain you or support your every decision. Nonetheless, let us continue with the false representations before we reach the real Jesus.

The Extraterrestrial Jesus

Now, this might sound strange to you. An Extraterrestrial Jesus? Surely not! Still, this is something which has surfaced time and time again.

You merely have to look up 'Jesus' and 'Extraterrestrial' as keywords in your browser to bring up a list of results pertaining to the many theories revolving around Jesus as an extraterrestrial. In some cases, people believe that Jesus was an alien from a neighboring planet or star system[5] who came to earth to interact with us and preach his cosmic knowledge - thus, not the son of God and the Messiah sent to forgive us for our sins.

In truth, this character is perhaps the least known of them all. This one is nevertheless an important piece of this puzzle. He is not from this world, instead of actually been born on earth from a virgin, this character lives on another planet and has visited earth on occasion just to give writings to the men that would become his prophets and spread a particular version of the gospel.

This Jesus is mostly made famous by the Church of Jesus Christ of Latter-Day Saints, a.k.a. the Mormon Church of the Latter-Day Saints. This character has evolved over the years and it's worth noting that he used to not like black people. Nowadays, though, he's cool with that. You read it right. This one evolves.

Another example of this character is the Flying Spaghetti Monster (FSM)[6], the purported deity of Pastafarianism - a now recognized religion which is nothing more than a mockery of the Savior. First created in order to discourage the teaching of intelligent design in schools, this Jesus peddle ridicule.

Its tenets are so ridiculous; it's clear that

they're satire, but this is still, in essence, a facet or representation of the Extraterrestrial Jesus. Naturally, this is so far from the truth it would be difficult to become confused about whether the FSM is Jesus or not.

Spoiler alert: He is not an extraterrestrial being.

In fact, by the time of this writing, yet another extraterrestrial Jesus showed up in the media. This was on a show called "The Orville" created by Seth MacFarlane (the creator of Family Guy).

This extraterrestrial character was presented as a woman name Kelly[7] who crashed on a less developed planet and used a dermoscaner to heal a little girl as the locals watched. Kelly then becomes a Jesus figure with churches, ministers, and everyone else willing to hang on every word spoken by Kelly and every myth created by her arrival on that planet.

It's interesting how the Jesus of Culture and the Extraterrestrial Jesus interlink. Driven by culture, these strange beliefs are centered around these characters and the people's rebelious desire to create and worship their own gods.

The Jesus of Politics

This Jesus was long ago appropriated by the politicians.

He shows up year after year as a means to gather votes and manipulate the masses into the utopia of this world. In the United States, he shows up on both sides of the spectrum, for Conservatives and Democrats. It seems that the Jesus of politics is bipartisan.

This Jesus is very dangerous, often distracting people from the actual gospel and turning his followers into compromising machines who are never interested in looking forward toward the Kingdom of God.

This Jesus is focused on short-term victories and often collides with his counterpart of the opposition party. This character isn't a savior but rather a mascot. He is a hardcore capitalist or an absolute communist, depending on where you personally stand on these issues. This Jesus may or may not have died on a cross, but for sure, he feeds the hungry, drinks barrels of wine, and hangs out with prostitutes.

The Jesus of Politics overlaps with the Jesus of Culture as when culture changes, so too does the politics of the time. So, this Jesus is OK with sin, abortion, and his followers not taking control of the city gates. This Jesus came to the world on a suicide mission assigned to him by his father.

If you've identified or encountered some of those Jesuses in your lifetime, you may feel confused. You may be thinking that they are all interpretations or misinterpretations of the real Jesus or you may be asking who is the real Jesus? Let's dive deeper and discover the truth.

"Only when you know the real item really well, you are able to spot a fake."
- Anonymous

The Jesus of Religion

This Jesus is the prophet, the saint, the unreachable God.

Far away, seated on a throne, he spills legalism and rules for you to follow. This character is all about elation, introspection, and wishful thinking. Some of his followers still have him on a cross, others believed that he fell several times while carrying his cross and something eventful or even magical happened during each of those stumbles.

This character is hard to relate to. He is not the only mediator between God the Father and mankind.

He tells you about God and states that he knows God, but he never claims to be God. Instead, he is portrayed as an exceptionally good man, a great example, and even a prophet of God. Just like other religious entities like Mohammed, Buddha, and Vishnu, he is the embodiment of wisdom with a dash of the supernatural. He is a good preacher who is full of charisma.

This character is even known by some to have Mary Magdalene as his unwedded wife. He is a character with good motives - but just a good man. This Jesus partially existed in history, but he himself is not what matters. His followers follow him for the enlightenment he brings. He is a Savior, but not a Lord.

The Jesus of the Bible

This Jesus is described in all of the versions and translations of the holy book and yes, there are distinct differences between them.

If you are an Evangelical Christian, by now you've already started wondering if buying and reading this book was a good idea, so let's dive deeper.

> *"Many will say to me on that day, 'Lord, Lord, did we not prophesy in your name and in your name drive out demons and in your name perform many miracles?' Then I will tell them plainly, 'I never knew you...'"*
>
> **Matthew 7:22-23**

From time to time, the characters above will try to influence and change who this Jesus is, what he does, why he exists, and how he relates to humanity. So, I find it very important to be precise here.

This Jesus is not the common denominator of all of his versions. This Jesus is not exclusive at all to the theologians. In fact, this Jesus will review himself to an illiterate fisherman with the same calling as he will to a doctor.

Jews and Gentiles alike will have an opportunity to know Him and he will always have your back no matter what. God the Father has placed everything in his hands, and it was with those hands that he washed the feet of his disciples.

This Jesus is different – he's always existed, yet he was born in flesh and blood. He never sinned, yet he carried all the sins of the world. He was, he is, and he is to come. No kidding, the enemy of humanity has tried hard to distort his image and distract people from who Jesus actually is.

Many will say, "Lord, Lord," but to them he will reply "I never knew you."

Were these folks following the wrong Jesus? Someone once said that "A fish is the last one to discover water." This means, if you are surrounded by something, culture, art, tradition, community, etc. and that is what consumes you, then you are most likely unaware of what transcends culture, art, tradition, community, etc.

You have eyes, but you don't see. The truth is in front of you, yet you are unable to grasp. When all you know is water and you swim in it all day, breathe in it all day, and go through life in it all day... that, my friend, is all you know.

PART TWO
Discovering Yeshua

What all these characters have in common is that they all borrow from Yeshua some historical facts. After all, these depictions didn't spring from nowhere – they are the creations of biased minds, working with what they believe they know about Yeshua... most of which is nonetheless incorrect. As a result, there are billions of people on this planet, and probably as many interpretations of Yeshua.

This is precisely why they are called facets or representations of Jesus. They are not representations of the true son of the almighty God, but rather fragments of human creation. They spring from factual historical events and are combined with a twisted ideology that God needs human help if He is to redeem humanity. These are distortions of the truth and not the truth itself, but you may have realized that by now.

Besides that, they can be summarized as depictions of a mystical, if not magical, creature... and yes, I mean "creature," as these interpretations were created by man to please man's desire for a God that can be boxed into a believable superhuman. This is an entity that can be easily processed, preached and followed.

In the end, as we have seen over and over, these mythical creatures can be easily rebuked and rebutted by any average atheist because they too have their own created gods.

This is why we must unpack the real Jesus. And His name isn't Jesus, but Yeshua.

When the almighty God was asked what his name was, he replied: "I AM". Likewise, when Yeshua presented himself, he presented himself as "I AM".

> *"Very truly I tell you,"* Jesus answered, *"before Abraham was born, I am!"*
> **John 8:58**

Based on who he says he is, we can establish that he is God and that the previous characters are not Yeshua, the son of the almighty God. Let's go further..

Most people have an idea of who Jesus Christ is. That's not the problem. The problem is that the idea that most people have of who Jesus Christ is is actually wrong. So let me break it down for you:

> *"When I was a child, I talked like a child, I thought like a child, I reasoned like a child. When I became a man, I put the ways of childhood behind me"*
> **1 Corinthians 13:11**

Let's start with the basics.

Jesus is known by his followers as the savior of the world, the King of Kings, the Lord of Lords, and so on and so forth, but who is this person we are talking about and why do we call him Jesus?

Let me explain:

History itself has reviewed that the name "Jesus" came to exist only in the last 500 years. It is a transliteration.

trans·lit·er·ate
trans'litəˌrāt,tranz'lidəˌrāt/
verb
write or print (a letter or word) using the closest corresponding letters of a different alphabet or language.

For non-linguistic majors, a transliteration means to replace the letters or characters of a word with the corresponding letter in another alphabet. The result of a transliteration preserves the form of the original, as distinct from a translation, which gives the equivalent word (often unrelated in form) in another language.

The name "Jesus" has been transliterated three times. From Hebrew to Greek, from Greek to Latin and from Latin to English, Spanish, Portuguese and other modern languages. From Yeshua to Iesous, from Iesous to Iesus and from Iesus to Jesus.

When a word is transliterated, it loses its original meaning, as a transliteration preserves only the form of the original. In essence, it means you're using English letters to sound out a foreign word. A translation, on the other hand, gives the equivalent word in another language. The name Jesus doesn't sound at all like the original word "Yeshua". Therefore, the name Jesus has no meaning in English, Iesus has no meaning in Latin and Iesous has no meaning in Greek. These names are just forms of the original word.

In fact, his Hebrew name Yeshua (see image 1) morphed into a Galilean Aramaic version that ultimately culminated in a near-contemporary Greek transcription.

At a later date, the Tiberian Hebrew, Eastern Syriac, and Western Syriac also contributed with their own attested pronunciations after the invention of vowel diacritic systems (500+ AD).

Early Arabic and later Christian Arabic also took their turn transcribing Yeshua's name. Not to be left behind, there is even a strange spelling of Yeshua's name found in the Qur'an.

This insatiable mashup of translation and transcription gets more and more complex, making it difficult to be verified and validated. Each of the thousands of sources and historians has their own personal bias and understanding of what the truth is. So, I ask:

Image 1. His Hebrew name.

His Hebrew name is Yeshua. His title is HaMashiach.

So, let me simplify it all for you.

His name is: Yeshua.
His title is: HaMashiach.

Who is he that I am talking about?

There are thousands of books written by very smart theologians and followers of the Messiah. So, I am not going to even attempt to provide a comprehensive essence of who he is. Still, it is important to understand who you are following because Yeshua is who defines your identity.

The person I am writing about is the Son of the Almighty God.

> *"If your messiah was a Hebrew why do you call him by a Greek name?"*
> — *Douglas DoNascimento*

The Meaning

We know that Yeshua was a Jewish man with a Jewish name and that this Jewish name has a meaning. In the Bible, names have meaning and it is for that reason that the son of the almighty God was named Yeshua. Yeshua is translated with the English word "salvation."

> *"She will give birth to a son, and you are to give him the name Yeshua, because he will save his people from their sins."*
> **Matthew 1:21**

Look at this way:
> *"She will give birth to a son, and you are to give him the name Salvation, because he will save his people from their sins."*
> **Matthew 1:21**

In essence, the angel was saying call him "Yeshua" because "he will save his people from their sins."

The name expresses his identity and his mission "because he will save his people from their sins" (Matthew 1:21), "Eight days later, when the baby was circumcised, he was named Yeshua, the name given him by the angel even before he was conceived" (Luke 2:21). Peter proclaimed that "there is no other name under heaven given to men by which we can be saved" (Acts 4:12).

So, if Yeshua means Salvation, why does it matter? Let's read the Bible and see just a few examples of where the word Yeshua shows up:

Genesis 49:18
"I have waited for your salvation, O Lord!"

Or

"I have waited for your YESHUA, O Lord!"

Exodus 15:2
"The Lord is my strength and song,
And He has become my salvation;
He is my God, and I will praise Him;
My father's God, and I will exalt Him."

Or

"The Lord is my strength and song,
And He has become my YESHUA;
He is my God, and I will praise Him;
My father's God, and I will exalt Him."

I Chronicles 16:23
"Sing to the Lord, all the earth;
Proclaim the good news of His salvation from day to day."

Or

"Sing to the Lord, all the earth;
Proclaim the good news of His YESHUA from day to day."

Psalm 3:8
"Salvation belongs to the Lord.
Your blessing is upon Your people. Selah"

Or

"YESHUA belongs to the Lord.
Your blessing is upon Your people. Selah"

Psalm 28:8
"The Lord is their strength,
And He is the saving refuge of His anointed."

Or

"The Lord is their strength,
And He is the YESHUA refuge of His MESSIAH."

Psalm 98:2
"The Lord has made known His salvation;
His righteousness He has revealed in the sight of the nations."

Or

"The Lord has made known His YESHUA;
His righteousness He has revealed in the sight of the nations."

Psalm 116:13
"I will take up the cup of salvation,
And call upon the name of the Lord."

Or

"I will take up the cup of YESHUA,

And call upon the name of the Lord."

(Please notice the correlation with Yeshua's words during passover when He said "This cup is the new covenant in My blood, which is shed for you." Luke 22:20)

Isaiah 12:2
*"Behold, God is my salvation,
I will trust and not be afraid;
'For Yah, the Lord, is my strength and song;
He also has become my salvation.' "*

Or

*"Behold, God is my YESHUA,
I will trust and not be afraid;
'For Yah, the Lord, is my strength and song;
He also has become my YESHUA.' "*

Isaiah 12:3
*"Therefore with joy you will draw water
From the wells of salvation."*

Or

*"Therefore with joy you will draw water
From the wells of YESHUA."*

(Please note that Yeshua said to the woman at the well: "but whoever drinks of the water that I shall give him will never thirst. But the water that I shall give him will become in him a fountain of water springing up into everlasting life."" John 4:14)

Isaiah 62:1
*"For Zion's sake I will not hold My peace,
And for Jerusalem's sake I will not rest,*

*Until her righteousness goes forth as brightness,
And her salvation as a lamp that burns."*

Or

*"For Zion's sake I will not hold My peace,
And for Jerusalem's sake I will not rest,
Until her righteousness goes forth as brightness,
And her YESHUA as a lamp that burns."*

(Please note "Nor do they light a lamp and put it under a basket, but on a lampstand, and it gives light to all who are in the house." Matthew 5:15)

Jonah 2:9

*"But I will sacrifice to You
With the voice of thanksgiving;
I will pay what I have vowed.
Salvation is of the Lord."*

Or

*"But I will sacrifice to You
With the voice of thanksgiving;
I will pay what I have vowed.
YESHUA is of the Lord."*

(Please note "But He answered and said to them, An evil and adulterous generation seeks after a sign, and no sign will be given to it except the sign of the prophet Jonah. For as Jonah was three days and three nights in the belly of the great fish, so will the Son of Man be three days and three nights in the heart of the earth." Matthew 12:39-40)

The word Yeshua appears 78 times in the old testament. The new testament would not be compiled for another 500 years. So, it is reasonable to conclude that the disciples witnessed what Yeshua said and did, comparing this with the prophecies in the scriptures available to them.

What about Christ?
So, what does "Christ" mean and why is Jesus called "Christ" in the first place?

As mentioned before, in Hebrew, Yeshua received the title of "The Messiah," which meant the "Anointed One".

The word "Christ" is a Greek translation of the word Messiah. In Hebrew, it translates as HaMashiach.

The title "HaMashiach" or "The Messiah" or "Anointed One" was given to Yeshua as he is consecrated by God and anointed by the Holy Spirit for his redeeming mission.

He is the Messiah awaited by Israel, sent into the world by the Father. Yeshua accepted the title of Messiah, but he made the meaning of the term clear: "come down from heaven" (John 3:13), crucified and then risen, he is the suffering servant "who gives his life as a ransom for the many" (Matthew 20:28).

The name "Christian" comes from the name Christ and the term Christianity.

The Man and his Jewishness

The Man

His skin was darkened by the sun and purity oozed

from his pores. Neither Twain, Shaw, Wharton, Sanburg, Lawrence, Chandler nor Woolf were able to accurately describe Him.

He didn't have to be cool or shocking to be effective. He didn't have millions of followers - at least, not at first. There was only twelve — mostly unknown, uneducated and non-influential folks. His power didn't come from His peers as His authority came from within Himself and His word.

> *"The Word became flesh and lived among us. We saw His glory, the glory as the One and Only Son from the Father, full of grace and truth."*
> **John 1:14**

Although the world experienced the proverbial dark and stormy night upon His death, his story didn't end there. Actually, it never ended, because it never had a beginning. In His story, the elements of mystery are easily identifiable and followed by the type of revelation that requires change. Change in one's self. Selfless change.

If you discovered that you have turned into the wrong person, he is the only change that can really fix that. Nothing compares because there is no comparison. There is no benchline to compare to. No baseline to start from. No requirements preceding and no prologs to be logged. He just is. He just does.

Not created, but the Creator.

There was no special beauty about Him. Unlike the stars portrayed by the media, he really became one of us, in flesh and bone. He experienced all of the temptations and had all of the opportunities, we currently have, to sin. Yet, He didn't. Not even once.

He is not to be mistaken with the many Jesuses created by man or the Jesus characters we grow up accustomed to seeing during Easter and Christmas.

This Yeshua, the Son of the Almighty God, who inspired the Bible, is a very different and unique person. He is the one who there's no one above, before or after Him. He is a person, not the universe, but rather the one who created the universe.

He is not a feeling, but the one who created all feelings. Being aligned with planetary intelligence is great, although it is not to be confused with experiencing Yeshua inside of you. This Yeshua I am speaking about is not typically mentioned, followed, or present in many religious organizations. But, He is present where he is presented, and where he is presented, he is experienced.

> *"For where two or three gather in my name, there am I with them."*
> **Matthew 18:20**

He is the creator of all things known and unknown. He was given a name, just like you and I, except that no man or woman gave him his name, God did. Because there was no one before him. He didn't have a beginning like the universe had a beginning – He is eternal and there are no words in the world that could fully describe Him, His love, His mercy or His grace toward us.

> *"He had no beauty or majesty to attract us to him, nothing in his appearance that we should desire him."*
> **Isaiah 53:2**

His Jewishness

"Then their eyes were opened and they recognized him, and he disappeared from their sight."
Luke 24:31

The gospel writer described here the all-so-common spiritual blindness and deafness. A condition that refers to the inability to see or hear the Son of God for whom He is.

"The God of this world has blinded the minds of those who do not believe."
2 Cor. 4:4

Once I had decided to write this book, I took a trip to Jerusalem, and while I was standing by the Wailing Wall, a rabbi approached me and asked: "Are you a Jew?" I responded - I don't know yet. But I do know that I follow a Jewish rabbi. He asked: "Who do you follow?" I replied, - Yeshua. He paused and with a confused look on his face, he said: "I never realized that Yeshua was a Jew." With a clear new realization in his eyes, he concluded: "Interesting…" My job there was done. If that divine appointment was the reason why God wanted me to be at that place, at that time, talking with that rabbi, I was fulfilled.

You see, Yeshua was a Jew and His truth has been so hidden by the falsities of this world, that people forget what the truth is. He was a Jewish man. And not only that, He was the only person to ever choose to be born as a Jew. Think about that. He could have chosen to be born anywhere in the world, under any set of circumstances and any culture. Yet, he chose Bethlehem in the region of Judah.

His choice didn't start when he was born. In fact, the entire Bible is his word and he chose the prophecies about him and the location where he was to be born. His objective was not to create a new religion, but rather to establish and point to "the way." Yeshua knew that He was going to become a Jewish man in order to fulfill God's plan for salvation.

> *"You Samaritans worship what you do not know; we worship what we do know, for salvation is from the Jews."*
> **John 4:22**

Or

> *"You Samaritans worship what you do not know; we worship what we do know, for YESHUA is from the Jews."*
> **John 4:22**

As mentioned previously, the name Yeshua means salvation.

Prophecies preceding Yeshua's arrival stated that He had to be from the line of King David and be eligible to be king of the Jews.

> *"After Jesus was born in Bethlehem in Judea, during the time of King Herod, Magi from the east came to Jerusalem and asked, "Where is the one who has been born king of the Jews? We saw his star when it rose and have come to worship him."*
> **Matthew 2:1-2**

He was so Jewish that the beginning of the New Testament starts with Matthew writing out Yeshua's lineage as the son of David and the son of Abraham.

> *"This is the genealogy of Yeshua HaMashiach the son of David, the son of Abraham"*
> **Matthew 1:1**

He was circumcised and later dedicated to the

temple. He was raised by practicing Jewish parents who observed Jewish law.

"When the time came for the purification rites required by the Law of Moses, Joseph and Mary took him to Jerusalem to present him to the Lord (as it is written in the Law of the Lord, 'Every firstborn male is to be consecrated to the Lord'), and to offer a sacrifice in keeping with what is said in the Law of the Lord: 'a pair of doves or two young pigeons.'"
Luke 2:22-24

He celebrated feasts like Passover every year.

"Every year Yeshua's parents went to Jerusalem for the Festival of the Passover."
Luke 2:41

He read and studied the Hebrew Bible - The Tanakh.

"And the child grew and became strong; he was filled with wisdom, and the grace of God was on him."
Luke 2:40

He was learning and teaching at the temple from a young age. This is a good indication that he was accustomed to His Father's house.

"After three days they found him in the temple courts, sitting among the teachers, listening to them and asking them questions. Everyone who heard him was amazed at his understanding and his answers."
Luke 2:46-47

He was recognized as a rabbi (a title of dignity given by the Jews to their doctors of the law and their distinguished teachers) by many (Matthew 19:16; 22:35-36; Luke 12:13). This is not an easy title to obtain. Yeshua was recognized with this title by the people as well as some leaders, such as, Pharisee Nicodemus.

> "Now there was a Pharisee, a man named Nicodemus who was a member of the Jewish ruling council. He came to Yeshua at night and said, 'Rabbi, we know that you are a teacher who has come from God. For no one could perform the signs you are doing if God were not with him.'"
> **John 3:1-2**

He was the fulfillment of that Law.

> "Do not think that I have come to abolish the Law or the Prophets; I have not come to abolish them but to fulfill them."
> **Matthew 5:17**

He had to die as the king of the Jews.

> "Pilate had a notice prepared and fastened to the cross. It read: Jesus of Nazareth, the king of the Jews. Many of the Jews read this sign, for the place where Jesus was crucified was near the city, and the sign was written in Aramaic, Latin and Greek."
> **John 19:19-20**

After his resurrection, He announced that he had to go so that the Holy Spirit could come.

> "But the Advocate, the Holy Spirit, whom the Father will send in my name, will teach you all things and will remind you of everything I have said to you."
> **John 14:26**

> "But very truly I tell you, it is for your good that I am going away. Unless I go away, the Advocate will not come to you; but if I go, I will send him to you."
> **John 16:7**

And the Holy Spirit came during the Jewish feast called Shavuot. This has immense importance, as

Shavuot is the feast that celebrates the arrival of the law of God - The Torah and commemorates the firstfruits of the harvest. Many Christians think of that day by the Greek term "Pentecost" (which translated means "50th day") without realizing the deeper meaning of the arrival of the Torah and the Holy Spirit of God on Earth.

After Yeshua arrived in Heaven, He continued to be referred to as from the tribe of Judah - his chosen Earthly birthplace.

> *"Do not weep! See, the Lion of the tribe of Judah, the root of David, has triumphed. He is able to open the scroll and its seven seals."*
> **Revelation 5:5**

So, from one of the first prophecies recorded on Genesis 49:10 "The scepter will not depart from Judah" to Yeshua's arrival on Earth, His life, death, resurrection, return to heaven and his promised second coming to Earth, Yeshua's Jewishness is a constant reminder of who he is.

Yeshua did not just happen to be born Jewish. His Jewishness is not to be ignored as a mere footnote. Christians by definition are followers of Christ. Christ means "Messiah" and "Anointed one." Christ is the Greek word for HaMashiach.

So, my questions to you are: How can you claim to follow the son of the Almighty God, Yeshua HaMashiach (Jesus Christ) and ignore all of the examples He himself gave on Earth?

> *"Whoever claims to live in him must live as Yeshua did."*
> **1 John 2:6**

Are you sure you are following the son of the Almighty God? Or perhaps, you have been following the sanitized version of Him. The Jewish-free version. An adaptation that sets Judaism as a separate religion, with a separate God. Are you ignoring the real savior?

The Perception

Understanding Yeshua encompasses understanding how those around Him perceived Him, the culture he chose to be a part of and the context, in which, the Scriptures about Him, were written.

> "His people were unwelcoming toward Him and now the world can't exist without Him."
> - Chuck Missler

He suffered rejection so that we could become His friends. He fulfilled over 400 prophecies from the Old Testament with his life. He never was. He always is. He never needed to self-examine. He knew no regrets and he made the ultimate sacrifice for those who had doubted Him, who had feared Him, and who had scorned Him.

His understanding, his power, and his glory were far beyond the comprehension of those who walked with him. Yet, his life exemplified how God sees us and His desire to be near us.

The world cannot exist without Yeshua. You and I cannot exist without Him.

Throughout all of this, He never looked at us as creatures, but instead as brothers and sisters. As co-heirs with him in His house, He invited us to sit at His table and eat with Him.

Those witnesses who were close to Him, likely had their own misconceptions… for who could truly comprehend all of his glory before it was truly revealed to them?

Those who doubted Him were proved wrong. Nonetheless, he never took pleasure in their falsities.

He is our performing high priest and our reigning King, the King of Glory, the King of Kings, the Lord of Lords, the King of the ages, the King of heaven, the King of the Jews, the King from the line of David and the King of Israel. Yet, his Kingdom was not of this World.

His reign is righteous. His goodness is limitless. His mercy is everlasting. His grace is sufficient.

He is indescribable, incomprehensible, irresistible and invincible.

He had it all and he gave it up so that he could give it all to us.

His backstory was like that of no one else, yet everyone else talked about His history. A history with no predecessor and no successor. A history that has always been and will always be. The heavens cannot contain him, and man cannot explain him. Herod couldn't kill Him, death couldn't handle Him and the grave couldn't hold Him.

He was a prophet before Moses and a champion before Joshua, an offering in place of Isaac and a wise counselor above Solomon. The one who placed the stars in the skies and called them by name was given all of the power and dominion forever and ever.

The heavens declare his glory and the firmament shows his handiwork. By Him were all things made and without Him was not anything made. All things are held together By Him.

Yet, he humbled himself, so that we could be lifted up. He became a servant so that we could be made co-heirs. He denied Himself so that we could freely receive all things. He who is, who was and who always will be, the first and the last, the Alpha and Omega, the conqueror of Jericho, the Kinsman-Redeemer and our Avenger of Blood, impartially merciful, Eternal and imperially powerful.

And the kicker is that He gave himself such power because only He had it to give. Throughout mankind's history, pivotal scenes pressed upon us because of their importance and our necessity to live. Those scenes told us stories and communicated to us in ways we could understand, the mysteries that are beyond us.

The principles that hold it all together were presented for our benefit and point to a single source we call the redeemer, the lamb of God, the mediator, Wonderful Counselor, Prince of Peace, the shepherd who is the Savior of the World.

"He was crucified on a cross of wood, yet He made the hill on which it stood."
- Chuck Missler

His name is Yeshua.
He is The Messiah.

His name exists from the very first verse "In the Beginning God created the heavens and the earth" Genesis (1:1) to the very last verse in "The grace of the Lord Yeshua be with Yahweh's people. Amen" (Revelations 22:21) and everywhere in between.

And to His holy name. The name above all names,

every knee shall bow and every tongue shall confess that Yeshua is Lord! His is the kingdom, the power, and the glory... forever, and ever. Amen.

The Essence of His Purpose

"Yeshua's essence is that He and He alone is the savior."
- Douglas DoNascimento

Unlike the flashing Jesus characters and their characteristics, Yeshua is truly and completely different. He hovers around us. He protects us like a lion protects its cub. He is personable because he is a person. He will guide you when you need guidance, forgive you when you repent, strengthen you when you need strength, and reward you when you are diligent.

His love for you never changes and that love endures forever.

No matter how many characters are created by man, none can truly detract from or personify who Yeshua truly is – they cannot capture his essence. They do not represent his presence, and that is precisely why they are false representations of Him.

They are false idols.

And truly, what agreement is there between the temple of God and idols? For we are the temple of the living God.

As God has said:
"I will live with them and walk among them, and I will be their God, and they will be my people. Therefore, Come out from them and be separate, says the Lord. Touch no unclean thing, and I will receive you. And, I

will be a Father to you, and you will be my sons and daughters, says the Lord Almighty."
2 Corinthians 6:16-18

Can you see the difference between the real Yeshua and those characters which have been shown to you, and, in some cases, forced upon you?

I caution you - do not be fooled by these false characterizations. Do not be drawn in by wickedness and fall into the trap of those enemies who wish nothing but to impose these falsehoods on you.

Yeshua is not an item or picture to be sold. He is not a book. He is not a myth or a zealot. Nor is he the symbol of the cross or the blood on the Shroud of Turin. He is not political and he is not cultural. He is not any single thing, yet every knee will bow to him.

He truly is the truth, the way, and the light.

You must ask yourself:
What are you going to do about it?

Now that you know about the false idols, the man made characters they call Jesus, I call on you to make your decision – to repent and turn away from your wicked ways.

This is what the entire journey to find and accept the real Yeshua is all about. Here is the truth laid bare for you:

Yeshua wants to have a personal relationship with you forever.

But there is a problem...

Your sin - your failure to live by God's standards -

separates you from God.

God is holy. "All have sinned and fall short of the glory of God." (Romans 3:23) The penalty for sin is separation from God. You can't earn your way to his presence by being good, going to church or being baptized.

> *"For it is by grace you have been saved, through faith—and this is not from yourselves, it is the gift of God— not by works, so that no one can boast."*
> **Ephesians 2:8-9**

The solution you seek is...

Yeshua.

> *"For God so loved the world that he gave his one and only Son, that whoever believes in him shall not perish but have eternal life"*
> **John 3:16**

So, that's it. Yeshua (Yahweh saves) is the solution. Read the prayer below and if you agree with what it says, read it out loud. Allow your words to be a proclamation.

Lord Yeshua, I ask You to forgive my sins and save me from eternal separation from God. I believe and accept that Your work and death on the cross is sufficient payment for my sins. I accept you as my Lord and Savior. Amen.

Understand that no prayer devised by man is a substitute to repentance. Now, if you repented from your sins and accepted Yeshua as your Lord and Savior it's time to celebrate.

Yeshua has provided the way for you to know Him and to have a relationship with your heavenly Father. Through your faith in Yeshua, you have eternal life. God will hear your prayers and love you unconditionally. Ask him for strength and he will give you strength; wisdom and he will give you wisdom. Stay determined to walk in the center of his will and Yeshua will never leave you or forsake you.

Read the Bible. Join a local Christian church or small group and keep on reading the Bible and praying. The Bible is your compass - remember this in times of trouble, for surely there will be tests along the way.

"...Salvation is found in no one else, for there is no other name under heaven given to mankind by which we must be saved"

Acts 4:12

Final thought:

Although I prefer to call my Lord and Savior by his actual name - Yeshua. There is nothing specifically wrong in calling him by the Greek transliterated name "Jesus." However, in the Bible, names have meaning. The Greek, Latin and English name "Jesus" does not carry any intrinsic meaning. Therefore, I call him by his Hebrew name. Yeshua means salvation and his name is salvation.

Yeshua's mercy and grace will extend to any person, even if they choose to call him by another name. God understands that ignorance exists and people in different cultures may choose to call Yeshua by a culturally localized name. His power is not in the correct pronunciation of His name, but in the person to whom it refers.

His power is not in the correct pronounciation of His name, but in the person to whom it refers.

Still, if you prefer to call him by his actual name given by the almighty God: Yeshua is the Name Above All Names.

Amen.

REFERENCES

1. Leonardo da Vinci Painting Sells for $450.3 Million, Shattering Auction Highs (2017, November 5) Retrieved from https://www.nytimes.com/2017/11/15/arts/design/leonardo-da-vinci-salvator-mundi-christies-auction.html

2. 20 Great Books About Jesus Christ- and a free book offer. Limited Time Only! (2017, September 11) Retrieved from https://www.heartsandmindsbooks.com/2017/09/list-of-great-books-about-jesus-christ-and-a-free-book-offer-limited-time-only/

3. Examples of How Jesus Has Been Pictured Throughout History. (n.d.) Retrieved from https://www.loyolapress.com/our-catholic-faith/family/catholic-teens/religious-art/how-jesus-has-been-pictured-throughout-history

4. Turin Shroud: "Blood" Still Fake. (2017, July 28) Retrieved from http://www.centerforinquiry.net/blogs/entry/turin_shroud_blood_still_fake/

5. Was Jesus An Extraterrestrial Or Possibly An Anunnaki Hybrid? (2015, June 13) Retrieved from http://in5d.com/jesus-extraterrestrial-anunnaki-hybrid/

6. Flying Spaghetti Monster (n.d.) Retrieved from https://en.wikipedia.org/wiki/Flying_Spaghetti_Monster

7. Church of Kelly (n.d.) Retrieved from http://orville.wikia.com/wiki/Church_of_Kelly

www.ingramcontent.com/pod-product-compliance
Lightning Source LLC
Chambersburg PA
CBHW021133080526
44587CB00012B/1270